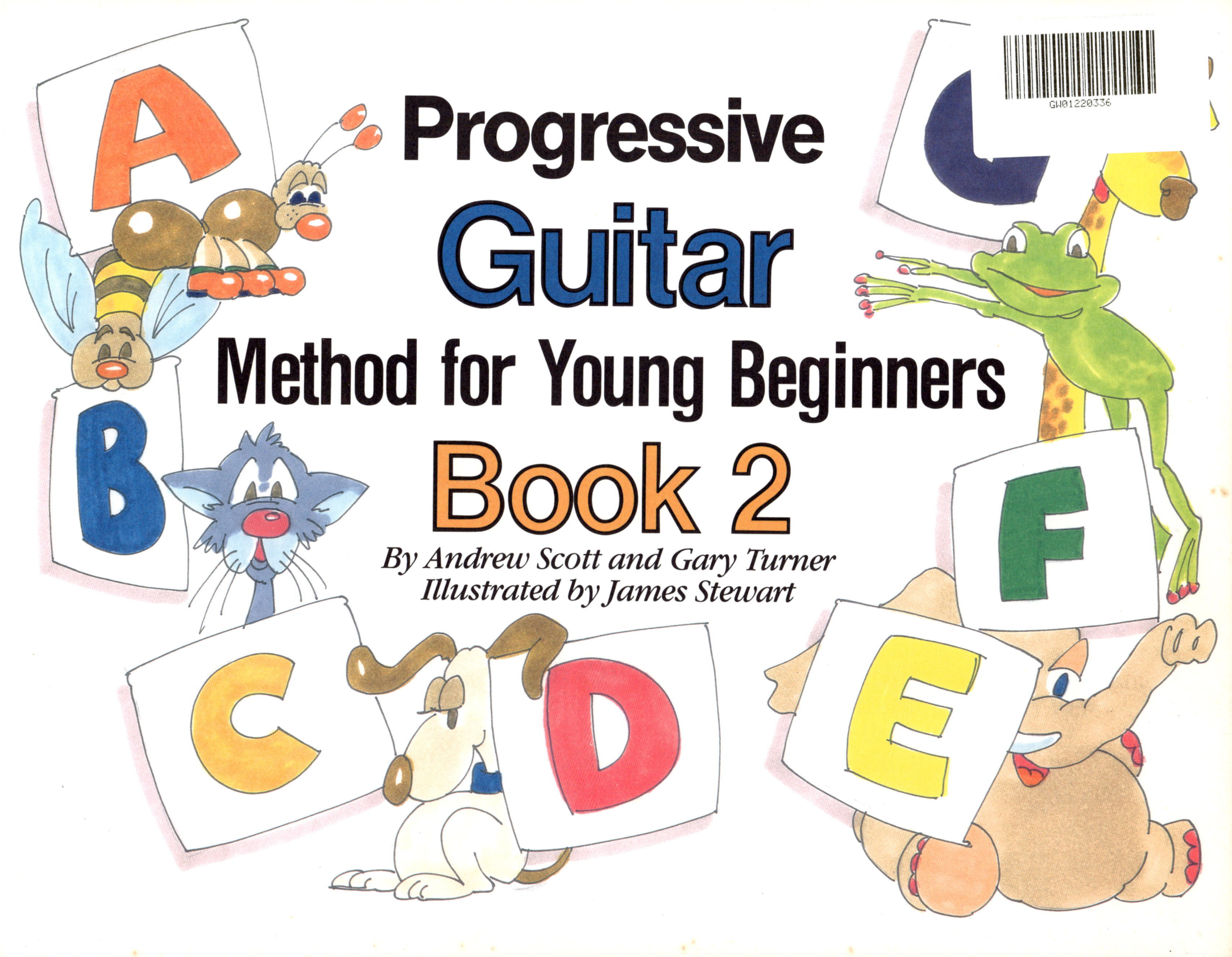

Let's Practice Together

We have recorded all the songs in this book onto a stereo cassette. When your teacher's not there, instead of practicing by yourself, you can play along with us. Playing will be much more fun, and you will learn faster. On the tape, each song is played on the right hand channel. An accompaniment (to play along with) is on the left hand channel. Each song is played four times.
- The first two times contain the song with the accompaniment.
- The third and fourth times contain just the accompaniment.
- A drum is used to begin each exercise and to help you keep time.

Tuning
To play along with the songs on the cassette, your guitar must be **in tune** with the guitar on the cassette. Ask your teacher to help you tune your guitar.

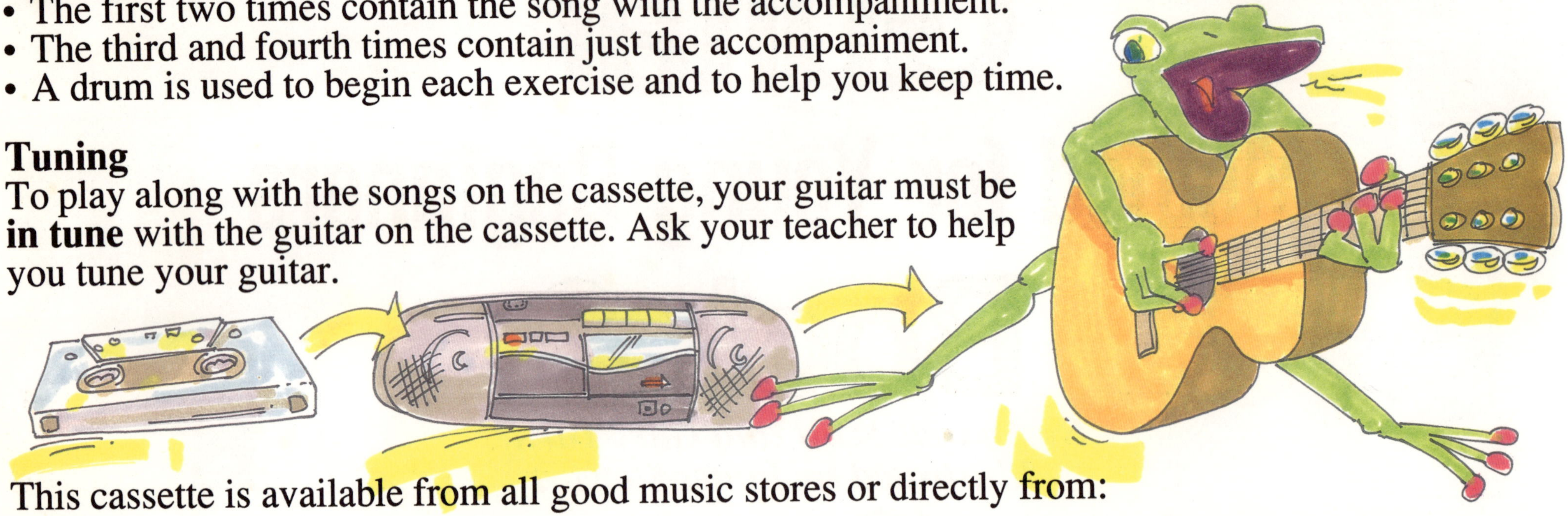

This cassette is available from all good music stores or directly from:

Australia – $14.95
Koala Publications
4 Captain Cook Ave.
Flinders Park 5025
South Australia
Ph. (08) 268 1750

U.K. & Europe – £6.25
(includes V.A.T.)
Music Exchange,
Mail Order Dept.
Claverton Rd,
Wythenshawe
Manchester M23 9NE
Ph (061) 946 1234

U.S.A. – $9.99
(Ca residents add tax)
Koala Publications Inc.
3001 Redhill Ave.
Bldg 2 #104,
Costa Mesa
CA. 92626
Ph. (714) 546 2743

If ordering direct please add $1.00 or 50p. postage per item. Payment by cheque or money order.

Contents

Introduction		Page 4
Lesson 1		**Page 5**
The Note E		5
Pop Goes the Weasel		5
For He's a Jolly Good Fellow		6
Lesson 2		**Page 7**
The Note F		7
How Dry I Am		8
Lesson 3		**Page 9**
The Note G		9
Little Miss Muffet		9
Mary Ann		10
Lesson 4		**Page 11**
The Eighth Note		11
Shave and a Haircut		12
Hot Cross Buns		12
Lesson 5		**Page 13**
Eighth Note Strum Patterns		13
Ten Little Indians		14
This Old Man		15
I'm a Little Teapot		15
Michael Finnegan		16
Shortnin' Bread		17
Lesson 6		**Page 18**
The Dotted Quarter Note		18
The Muffin Man		18
London Bridge		19
Lesson 7		**Page 20**
1st and 2nd Endings		20
Home, Sweet Home		20
Jingle Bells		21
Lesson 8		**Page 22**
The Open D Note		22
The Farmer in the Dell		22
Brother John		23
Lesson 9		**Page 24**
The D Chord		24
Big Ben		24
Here We Go Round the Mulberry Bush		25
Lesson 10		**Page 26**
The Note F♯		26
The Caissons Go Rolling Along		27
Notes, Chords and Rests		28

Introduction

Progressive Guitar Method for Young Beginners, consisting of three instruction books and two supplementary song books, has been designed to introduce the younger student to the basics of guitar playing and reading music.

To maximise the students' enjoyment and interest, the Progressive Young Beginner series incorporates an extensive repertoire of well-known childrens' songs.

All the songs have been carefully graded into an easy-to-follow, lesson-by-lesson format, which assumes no prior knowledge of music or the guitar by the student. Chord symbols and easy strum patterns are provided above each song.

The two supplementary songbooks are co-ordinated with the method books to provide the student with many additional songs to play.

Method Book 2 extends the range of notes to cover more than one octave, involving five new notes (E, F, G, open D and F#), and five simplified chord shapes (G, D7, C, G7 and B). It contains very easy arrangements of over 20 songs, and introduces the student to eighth notes, eighth note strum patterns and dotted quarter notes.

New pieces of information are highlighted by color boxes, and color illustrations are used throughout to stimulate and maintain the students' interest. Further songs to play are available in Supplementary Songbook A.

Supplementary Songbook A has been designed to be used in conjunction with Method Book 2. It contains more than 25 additional songs, which are cross referenced to the lessons in Method Book 2.

Lesson 1

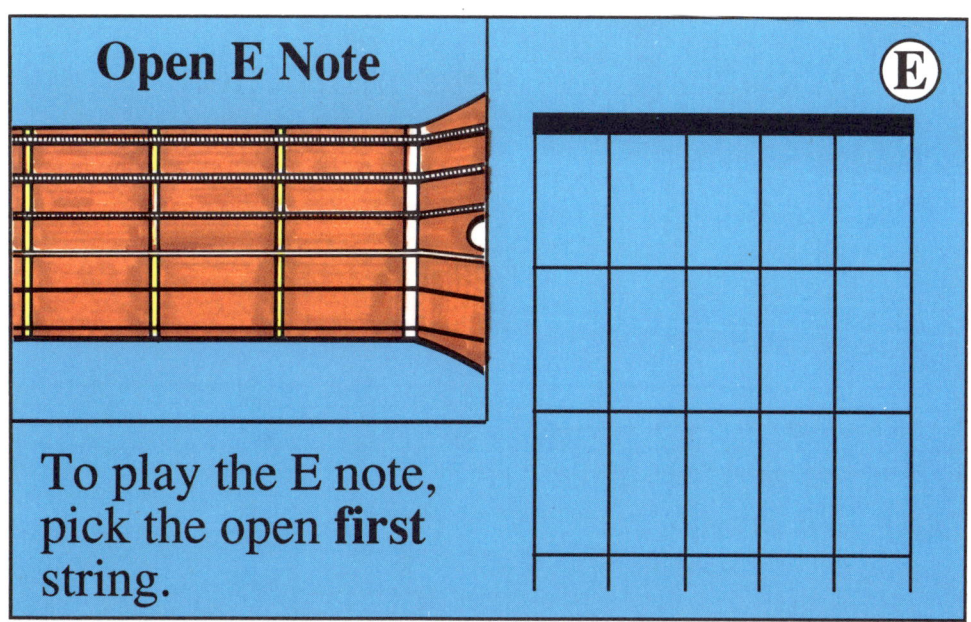

Open E Note

To play the E note, pick the open **first** string.

The Note E

E Note

This is an E note. The note E is written in the **fourth** space of the staff.

Strum Pattern

🎵 **Pop Goes the Weasel**

To play the rests in bar 13, stop the E note from sounding by lightly touching it with the first finger of your left hand.

Half a pound of tup-pen-y-rice, half a pound of trea-cle, mix them up and make it nice, Pop! goes the wea-sel.

For He's a Jolly Good Fellow

On the cassette there are **five** drumbeats to introduce this song.

Strum Pattern

V.
1 2 3

D.C. al Fine (pronounced "fee-nay")

Over bar 24 the instruction ***D.C. al Fine*** is written. This means that you play the song again from the beginning until you reach the word *Fine*.

[Sheet music in 3/4 time, key of G. Chord progression: G G C G D7 D7 G | G G G C C G D7 G (Fine) | G C G G G C G G (D.C. al Fine)]

Count: 1 2 3 1 2 For he's a jol-ly good fel - low, for he's a jol-ly good fel - low, for he's a jol-ly good fel - low, which no-bo-dy can de-ny. Which no-bod-y can de-ny, which no-bo-dy can de-ny.

You can now play the songs on pages 5 to 9 of Guitar Method for Young Beginners Supplementary Songbook A.

How Dry I Am

Strum Pattern

V		V	
1	2	3	4

On the cassette there are **five** drumbeats to introduce this song.

Count: 1 2 3 4 1 How dry I am, How dry I am,
No - bod - y knows, How dry I am.

Lesson 3

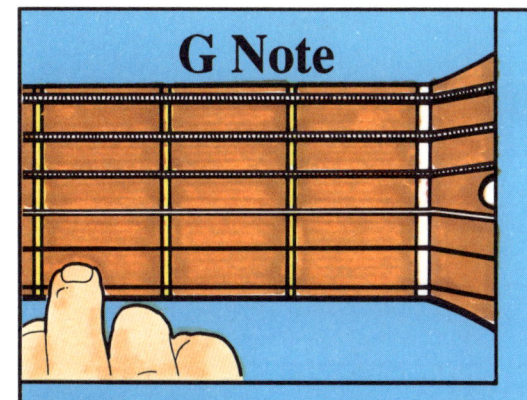

G Note

Play the G note with the **third** finger of your left hand just behind the **third** fret of the **first** string.

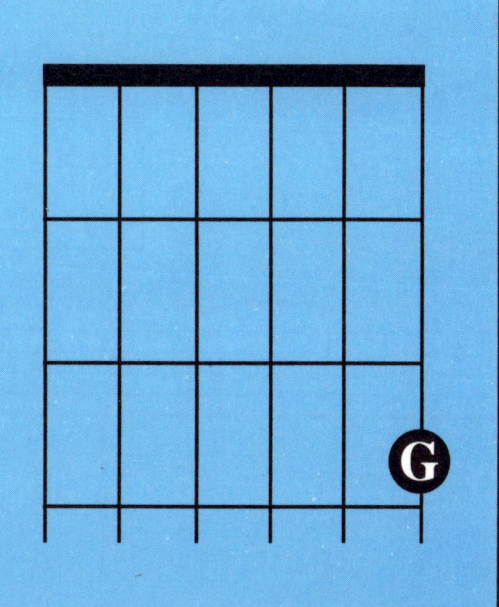

The Note G

G Note

This is a G note. The note G is written in the space above the staff.

Strum Pattern

 **Little Miss Muffet**

Little Miss Muffet sat on a tuffet, eating her curds and whey____, a long came a spider, who sat down beside her and frightened Miss Muffet away.

Two Bar Strum Patterns

So far all the strum patterns you have had are **one bar long**. In the song Mary Ann, use the following strum pattern which lasts for **two bars**.

Mary Ann

All day, all night Ma-ry Ann ____, down by the sea-shore, sift-ing sand ____. All the lit-tle chil-dren love Ma-ry Ann ____, down by the sea-shore sift-ing sand ____.

You can now play the songs on pages 10 and 11 of Guitar Method for Young Beginners Supplementary Songbook A.

Lesson 4

tail

This is an **eighth note**. It lasts for **half** a count. There are eight eighth notes in one bar of $\frac{4}{4}$ time.

The Eighth Note

When eighth notes are joined together, the tails are replaced by one beam.

Two eighth notes joined together.

Four eighth notes joined together.

🎧 How to Count Eighth Notes

Alternate Picking

All of the songs you have so far played involved a downward pick motion, indicated by **V**. With the introduction of eighth notes, down (**V**) and up (**∧**) picking is used. This is called **alternate picking**. In alternate picking, use a down pick **ON** the beat (the number count) and an up pick **OFF** the beat (the 'and' count). Try the following exercise:

🎧 Pieces of Eight

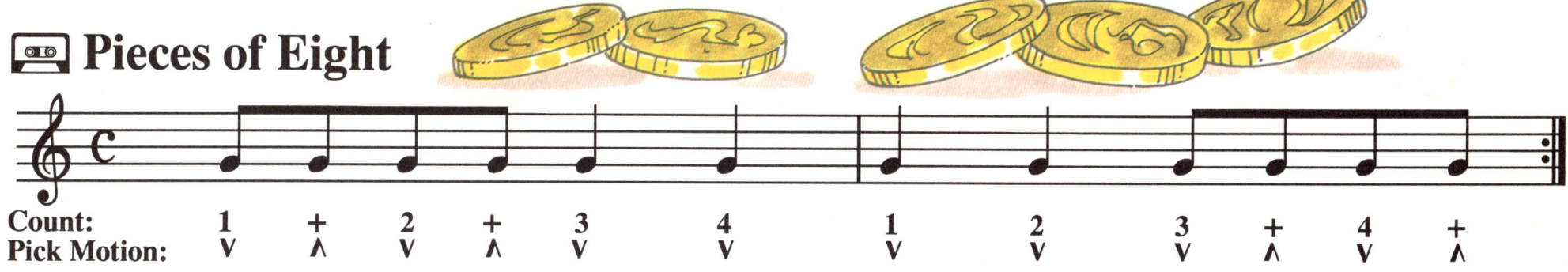

Shave and a Haircut

Use alternate picking on the second beat of the first bar. To achieve the rest on the first beat of bar 2, stop the third string from sounding by lightly touching it with your second finger.

Hot Cross Buns

You can now play the songs on pages 12 to 14 of Guitar Method for Young Beginners Supplementary Songbook A.

Lesson 5

Eighth Note Strum Patterns

All the strum patterns you have played so far involved playing a downward strum (V) on the first, second, third or fourth count. To make strumming more interesting, **eighth note** strum patterns can be used. An eighth note strum pattern uses a down and up strum within one count. An up strum is indicated by a ∧, and is played on the 'and' section of the count.

Play the following strum pattern, which has an up strum on the second beat.

Eighth Note Strum Pattern One

Practice this new strum pattern holding a G chord. Hold your pick lightly and strum evenly. When strumming, only move your wrist up and down. Do not move your arm. Play the following song using Eighth Note Strum Pattern Number One.

🎵 Up and Down Strum

Use Eighth Note Strum Pattern One when playing the chords of Ten Little Indians.

Ten Little Indians

| C | C | G7 | G7 |
One lit-tle two lit-tle three lit-tle In-di-ans, four lit-tle five lit-tle six lit-tle In-di-ans,

| C | C | G7 | C |
seven lit-tle eight lit-tle nine lit-tle In-di-ans, ten lit-tle In-di-an boys.

Eighth Note Strum Pattern Two

Practice playing Strum Pattern Two holding a G chord.

🎵 **This Old Man**

In this song use Eighth Note Strum Pattern Two.

This old man, he played one, he played nick nack on my drum, with a nick nack pad - dy whack give the dog a bone, this old man came rol - ling home.

Eighth Note Strum Pattern Three

Use Eighth Note Strum Pattern Three in the next song.

🎵 **I'm a Little Teapot**

I'm a lit - tle tea - pot, short and stout, here is my han - dle, here is my spout.

Eighth Note Strum Pattern Four

V∧ V∧ V V
1 + 2 + 3 4

Use Eighth Note Strum Pattern Four in the song Michael Finnegan.

🎵 Michael Finnegan

On the casssette there are **four** drumbeats to introduce this song.

Count: 1 2 3 4 There was an old man called Mi-chael Fin-ne-gan, he grew whi-skers on his chi-ni-gan, the wind came up and blew them in - a - gain, poor old Mi - chael Fin-ne-gan be-gin a-gain.

Two Bar Eighth Note Strum Patterns

On page 13, you were introduced to two-bar strum patterns. The two-bar strum pattern written below contains eighth note strums in the first bar (Strum Pattern Number Four), and half note strums in the second bar. Practice this new two-bar strum pattern holding a C chord. When you are confident playing it, apply it to the song Shortnin' Bread.

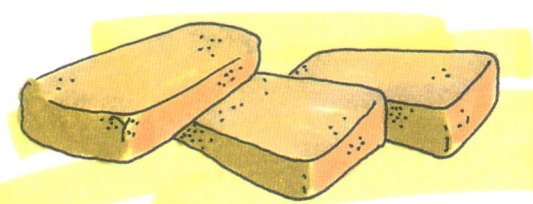
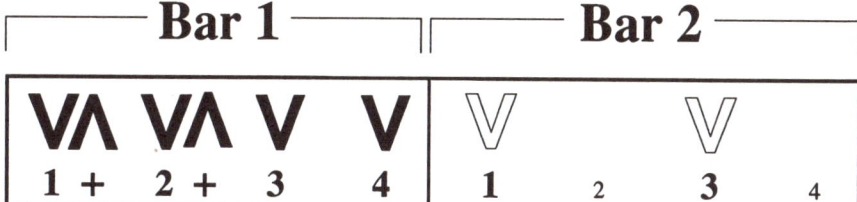

🎵 Shortnin' Bread

Bars 4 and 8 each contain two chords. Change to the second chord on the third beat of the bar. Also, in bars 4 and 8, to play the rest you must lightly touch the open third string with the second finger of your left hand, to stop it from sounding.

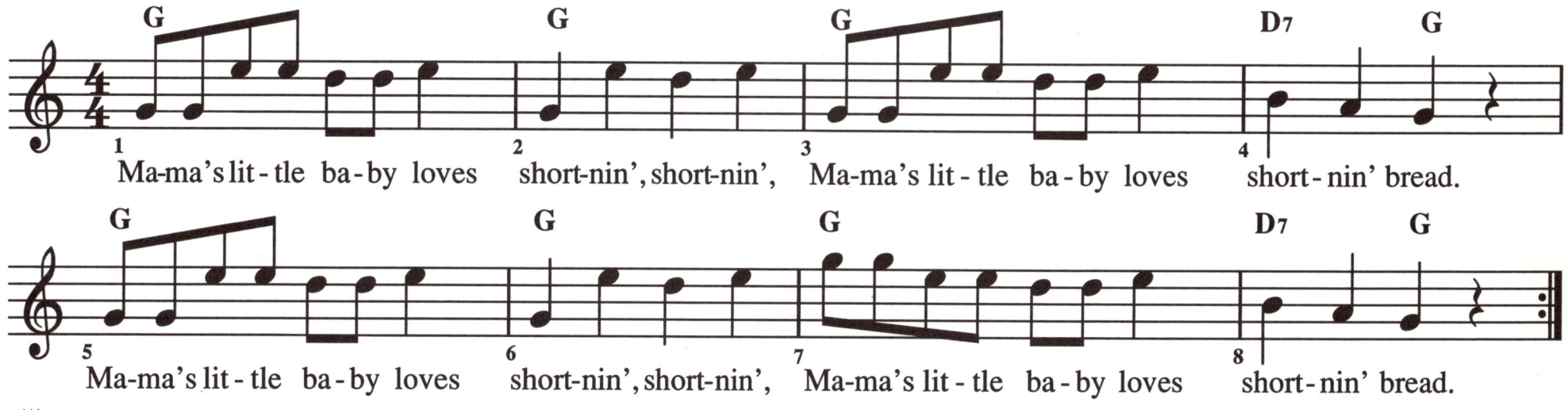

📖 You can now play the songs on pages 14 to 17 of Guitar Method for Young Beginners Supplementary Songbook A.

Lesson 6

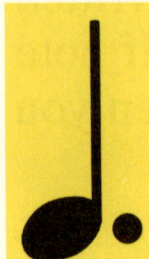

The Dotted Quarter Note

A dot written after a quarter note means that you hold the note for **one and a half** counts. A dotted quarter note is often followed by an eighth note.

Count: 1 2 + 3 4

Quarter Dot Rock

Strum Pattern

V∧	V∧	V	V
1 +	2 +	3	4

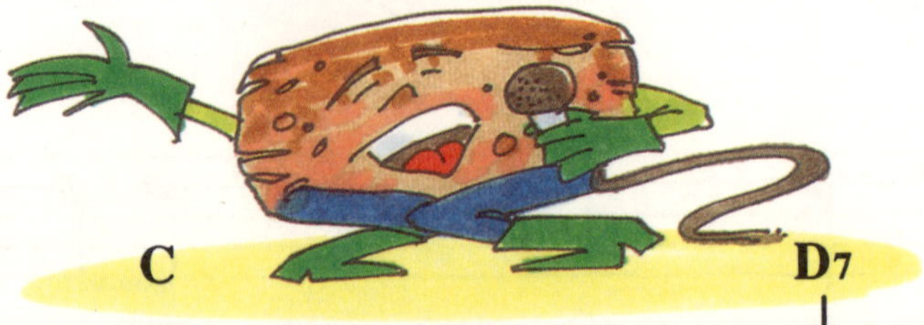

The Muffin Man

Strum Pattern

V		V	
1	2	3	4

Do you know the Muf-fin man, the muf-fin man, the muf-fin man?

Do you know the muf-fin man his wares are such a treat?

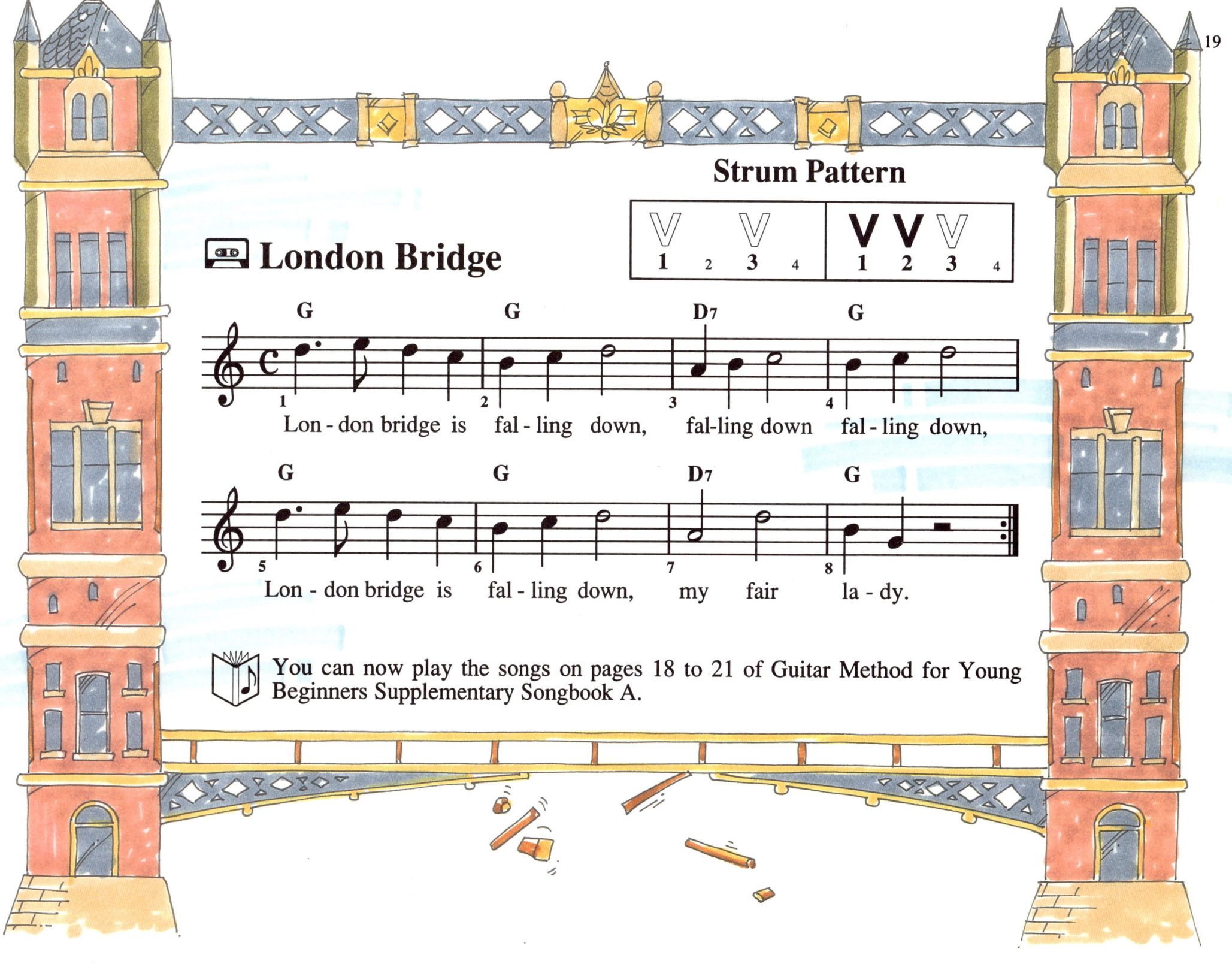

Lesson 7

First and Second Endings

The next two songs contain **first and second endings**. The first time you play through the song, play the first ending, (1.), then go back to the beginning. The second time you play through the song, play the second ending (2.) instead of the first.

First ending   **Second ending**

Strum Pattern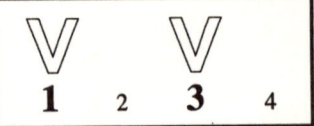

🎵 Home, Sweet Home

In this song, play through to the end of the first ending (bar 4), then repeat the song from the beginning, as indicated by the repeat dots. When you play through the song the second time, do not play bar 4 (the first ending), but play bar 5 (the second ending) instead. The repeat dots at the end of bar 5 indicate that the whole song is to be repeated. On the cassette there are **three** drumbeats to introduce this song.

Count: 1 2 3 O - ver moun - tains and val - leys where - e - ver you may roam,
Be it e - ver so hum - ble there's no___ place like home.

Jingle Bells

Strum Pattern: V V V
1   2   3   4

Jin-gle Bells, Jin-gle Bells, jin-gle all the way, O what fun it

is to ride on a one horse op-en sleigh, hey! one horse op-en sleigh.

Lesson 8

The Open D Note

D Note

This is the open D note. It is written in the space below the staff.

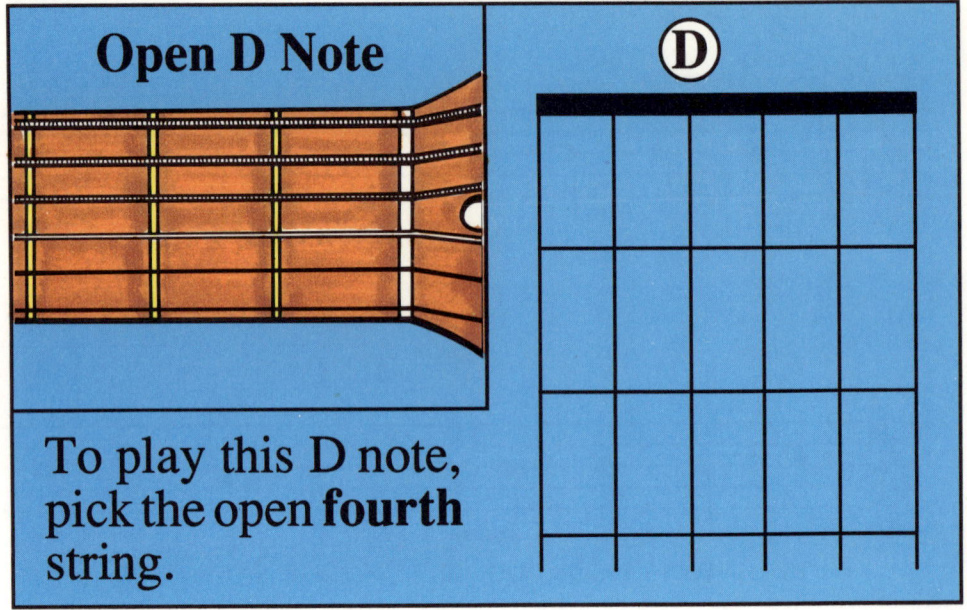

To play this D note, pick the open **fourth** string.

🎵 The Farmer in the Dell

On the cassette there are **five** drumbeats to introduce this song.

Strum Pattern

Count: 1 2 3 1 2 The far-mer in the dell____, The far-mer in the dell____, hi ho, the mer-ry O, the far-mer in the dell____.

🎵 Brother John

This song is a **round**. A round is a song where a second player can begin after the first has played a number of bars. In this song, the second player begins when the first player reaches bar 3.

To make the chords of this song more interesting, different strums are written above the staff.

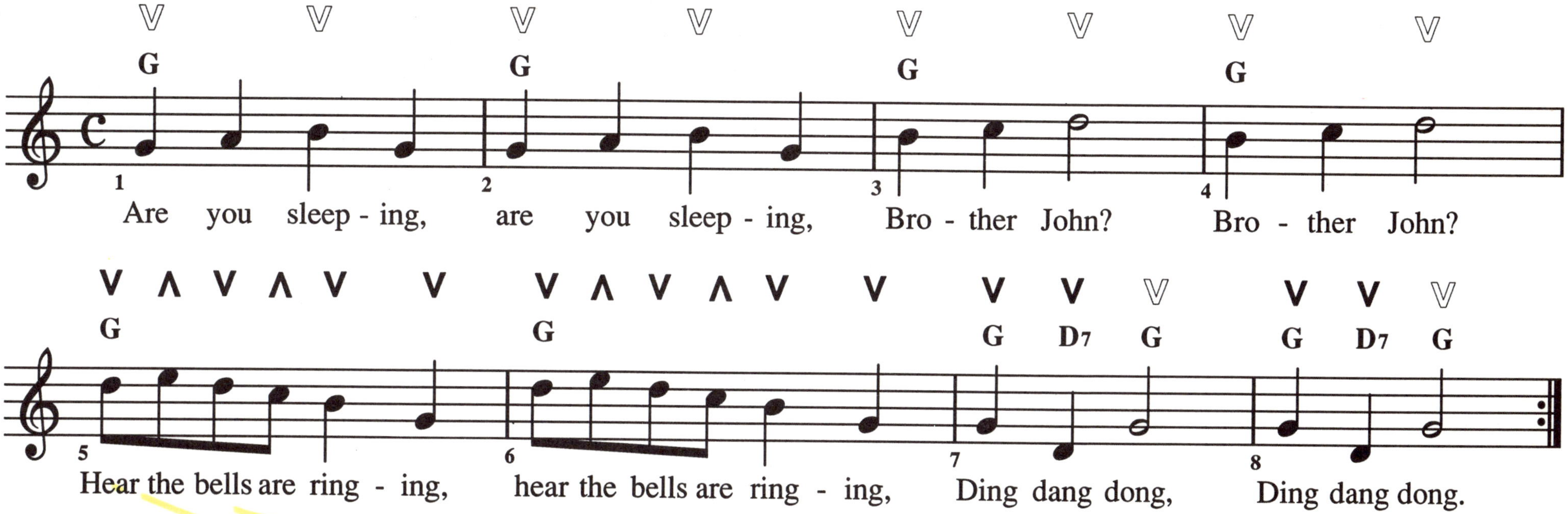

You can now play the songs on pages 22 to 24 of Guitar Method for Young Beginners Supplementary Songbook A.

Lesson 9

The D Chord

To play the D chord, use the **first, second** and **third** fingers of your left hand as shown in the diagram, but strum only **four** strings.

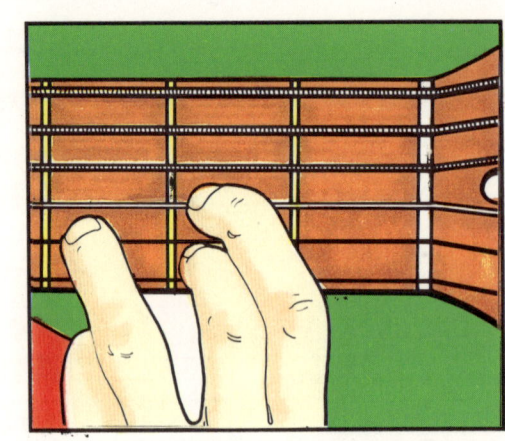
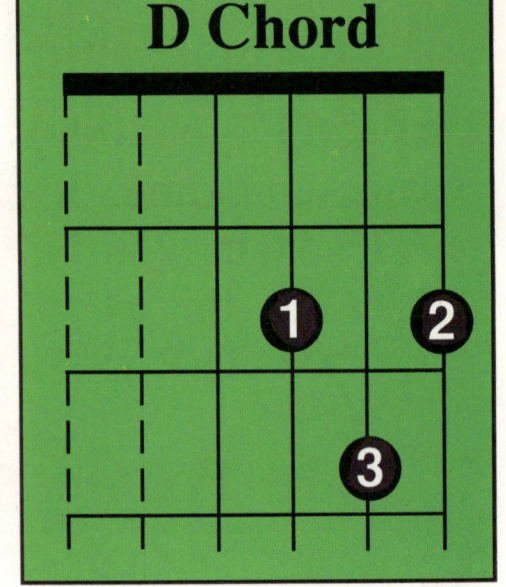

D Chord

Duck for Cover

Strum Pattern

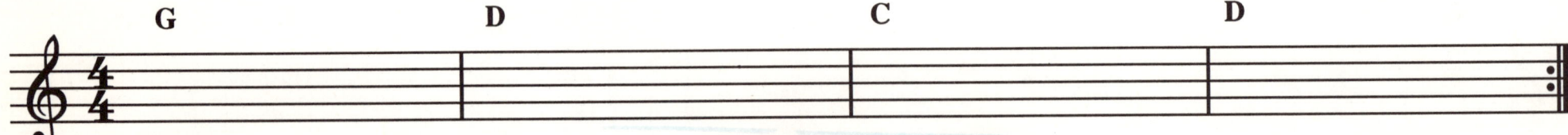

G   D   C   D

Big Ben

Strum Pattern

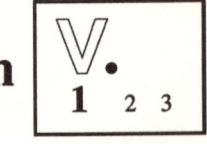

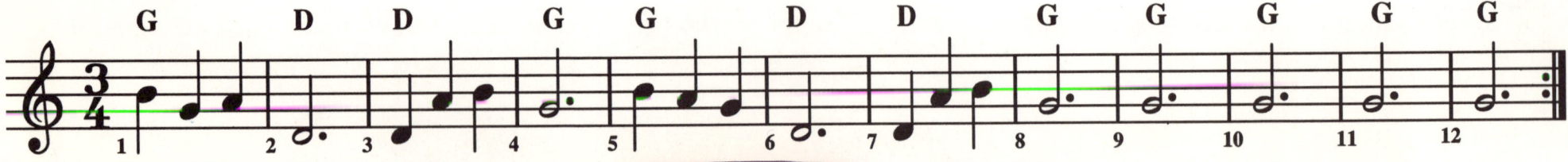

G D D G G D D G G G G G

Eighth Note Strum Patterns in 3/4 Time

On page 13 you were introduced to eighth note strum patterns in 4/4 time. Eighth note strum patterns can also be played in 3/4 time. Practice the following strum pattern, holding a G chord, then apply them to the song 'Here We Go Round the Mulberry Bush'.

Strum Pattern Number One

3/4 | V   V∧   V
    | 1   2 + 3

Here We Go Round the Mulberry Bush

Here we go round the mul-ber-ry bush, the mul-ber-ry bush, the mul-ber-ry bush. Here we go round the mul-ber-ry bush, on a cold and fros-ty morn-ing.

Lesson 10
The Note F Sharp (F#)

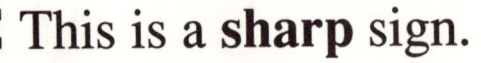 This is a **sharp** sign.

F# Note

A sharp sign written before a note on the staff means that you play the note that is one fret higher than the note written. Eg, the note written on the staff above is called F sharp (F#), and is played on the **second** fret of the **first** string. When a sharp sign is written on the staff, it is always written **before** a note.

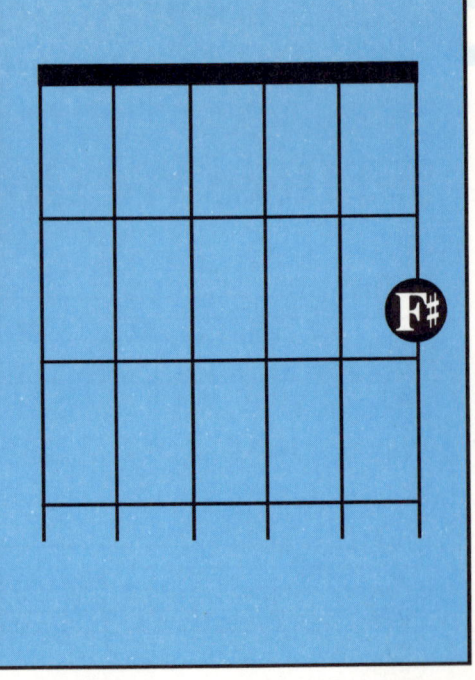

To play the note F#, place your **second** finger just behind the **second** fret of the **first** string.

Strum Pattern

🎵 **Autumn's Theme**

Instead of writing a sharp sign before every F♯ note on the staff, it is easier to write just one sharp sign after the treble clef. This means that all the F notes on the staff are played as F♯, even though there is no sharp sign placed before them.

The Caissons Go Rolling Along

On the cassette the are **six** drumbeats to introduce this song.

You can now play the songs on pages 25 to 28 of Guitar Method for Young Beginners Supplementary Songbook A.

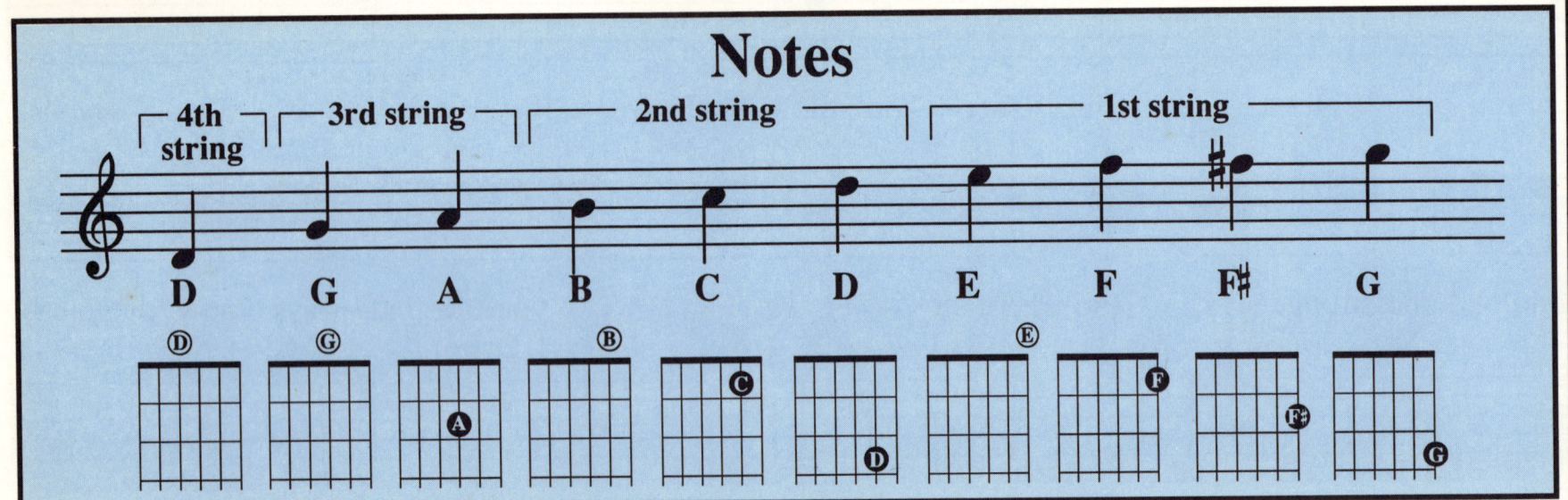
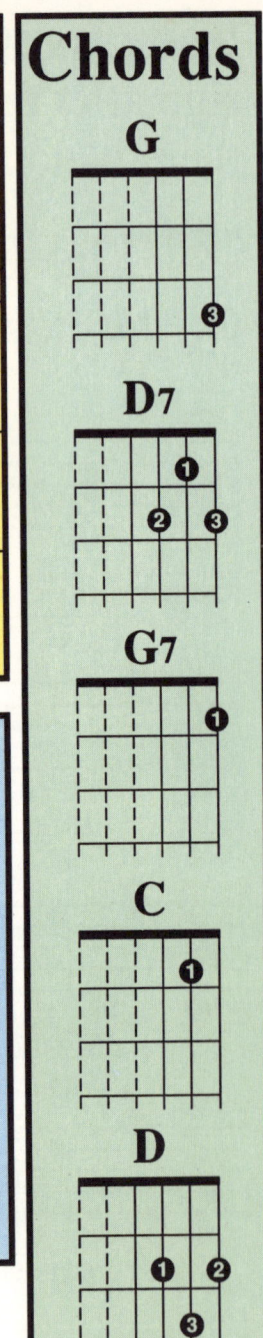

Proceed to Book Three